W9-DJI-899

THE CHANGING FACE OF
EGYPT

Text by RON RAGSDALE
Photographs by DANA SMILLIE

A Harcourt Company

Austin New York
www.raintreesteckvaughn.com

Published by Raintree Steck-Vaughn Publishers, an imprint of Steck-Vaughn Company

Library of Congress Cataloging-in-Publication Data is available upon request.

ISBN: 0-7398-5488-7

Printed in Hong Kong. Bound in the United States.

1 2 3 4 5 6 7 8 9 0 LB 07 06 05 04 03 02

Acknowledgments

The publishers would like to thank the following for their contributions to this book: Rob Bowden–statistical research; Nick Hawken–illustrations on pages 7, 18, 24, 30, 34, 40, 42; Peter Bull–map on page 5. All photographs are by Dana Smillie.

Contents

1 Cairo: Mother of the World

In the 15th-century tales of *1001 Arabian Nights*, which included "Aladdin" and "Ali Baba and the Forty Thieves," Cairo was called "the Mother of the World." It was given this name because it was thought to be the oldest and largest city on earth. Even then, it was already more than 4,500 years old. Today, Cairo is still the largest city in Africa and the Middle East.

In 1960, Cairo's population was 3.3 million, compared to 14.5 million today. The rapid development of housing, shopping centers, businesses, and schools has been accompanied by increasing pollution, noise, traffic, and general congestion. However, the city is doing its best to keep pace, with improved roads, a world-class subway system, and laws to combat pollution. Much of the old city, with its hundreds of medieval mosques, is being restored, especially since a major earthquake in 1992 damaged many of Cairo's architectural treasures.

Over the past 30 years, Cairo has become the center of the hugely popular Arab film and music industries, making Egyptian Arabic the most commonly understood dialect throughout the Arab world. Cairo is a fast-growing and diverse city, with many opportunities and challenges in the century ahead.

▲ *Old Cairo is a maze of winding streets, minarets, and hidden courtyards.*

◀ *Despite an improving public transportation system, the streets of Cairo are constantly congested with traffic.*

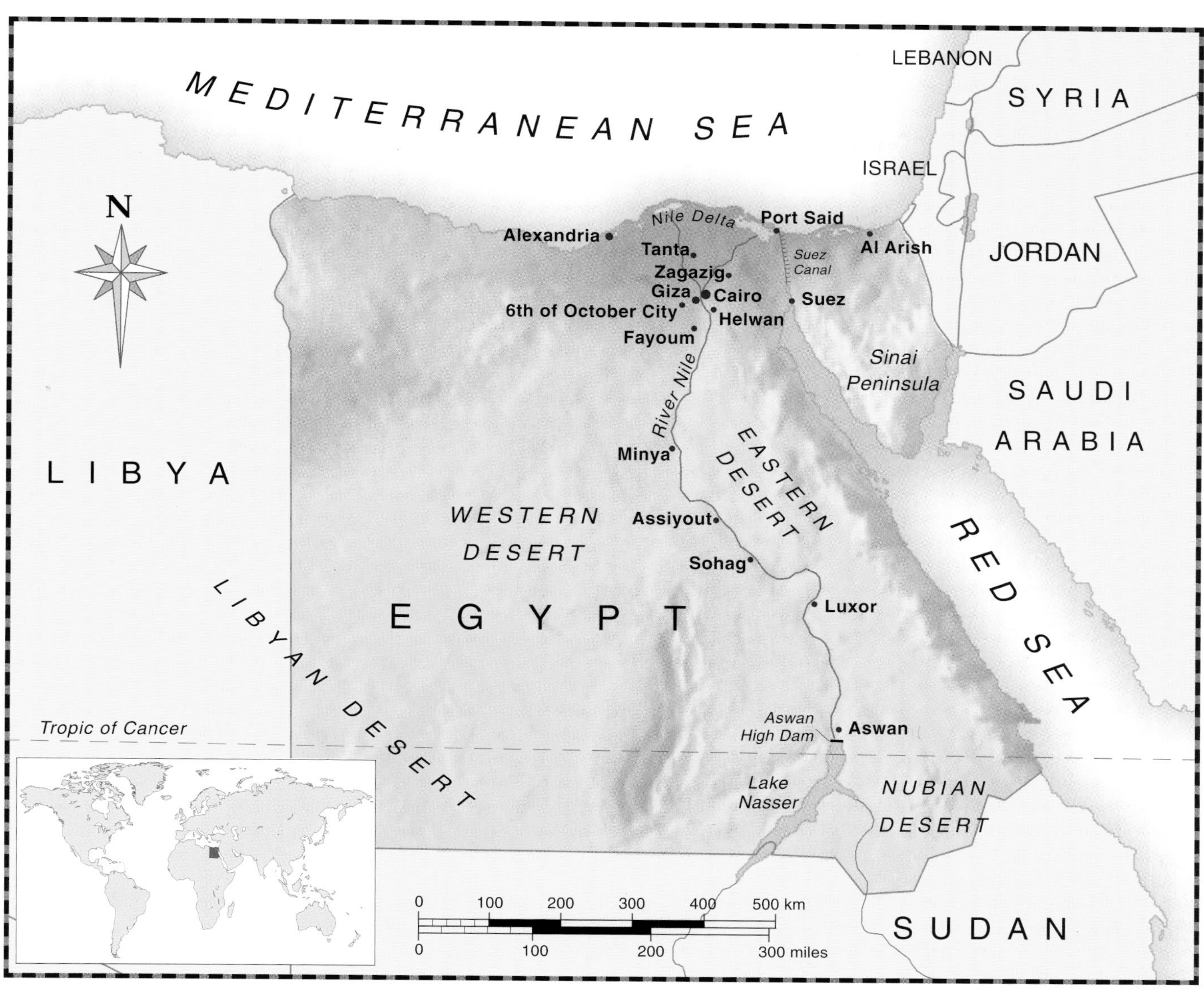

▲ *A map of the main geographical features of Egypt and places mentioned in this book.*

EGYPT: KEY FACTS

Area: 386,670 square miles (1,001,450 sq km)
Population: 68.47 million (2001)
Population density: 177 persons per square mile (5,935 per square mile in the Nile Valley)
Capital city: Cairo (metropolitan area, 14.5 million)
Other main city: Alexandria (3.4 million)
Highest mountain: Gebel Katherina, 8,670 feet (2,642 m)
Longest river: Nile, total length, 4,160 miles (6,695 km)
Main language: Egyptian Arabic
Major religions: Sunni Islam (94 percent), Christianity—mainly Coptic (6 percent)
Money: Egyptian Pound (gineh) (4.64 pounds = 1 dollar)

2 Past Times

For thousands of years, monsoon rains in the mountains of Ethiopia caused the Nile River to flood, delivering rich black silt into the desert. This made the Nile Valley the richest agricultural land in the world. The pharaohs of ancient Egypt took advantage of the regular floods and created a religious government with themselves as gods, who were said to control the rise and fall of the river.

The pharaohs ruled for 2,000 years, but the reliable harvest made Egypt a land worth conquering. During the 3rd century B.C., the pharaohs were overthrown by the Greeks, who in turn were toppled by the Romans. For the next 2,000 years, one occupying force followed another. Then, in 1952, a revolution re-established Egyptian rule over Egypt, and the country became a socialist democracy with an elected parliament and president.

◄ *Abu Simbel temple was built somewhere around 1800 B.C., during the reign of the Pharaoh Rameses II (the Great). Its purpose was to instill terror in the Nubian tribes to the south of his empire.*

Economic Reform

The founding of Israel in the formerly Arab territory of Palestine in 1948 led to serious conflict between Israel and the Arab countries that surrounded it, including Egypt. In 1979, after many years of hostilities, Egyptian president Anwar Sadat became the first Arab leader to sign a peace treaty with Israel.

This led to the "open door" policy, which encouraged Egyptian firms to export to the West, and allowed foreign firms to invest in and import goods into Egypt.

Egypt's support of the Western Allied countries during the Gulf War of 1990–1991 led to the cancellation of much of its foreign debt. This made even more ambitious economic reforms possible, which have begun to transform urban Egypt into a consumer-oriented society. Meanwhile, many Egyptians continue to follow the very conservative agricultural and religious lives led by their ancestors.

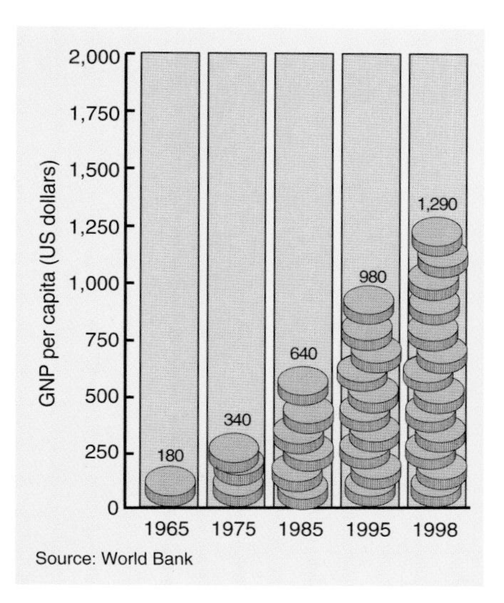

▲ *The changes in the Egyptian government's economic policy since 1965 have resulted in a dramatic rise in the country's gross national product.*

◀ *The pyramids that overlook the city of Giza are a constant reminder of Egypt's past.*

IN THEIR OWN WORDS

"My name is Reda Sobhi Wadiya and I'm 23 years old. I'm a line production manager at the Mobaco clothing factory. I live in Cairo, but I'm originally from Sohag in Upper Egypt. I came to Cairo in 1996 to study at Helwan University, and I stayed here for the good job opportunities.

"Egypt has changed a lot since my mother was young. I live in my own apartment in the Heliopolis district. I'm engaged to be married, but I'll definitely continue working after our wedding. Then, when I have children, I'll arrange for day care so I can keep working at my job. Although our country has an amazing history, I'm glad I have all the freedoms of today!"

3 Landscape and Climate

The Nile Valley

The Nile is the longest river in the world. It starts in central Africa and flows more than 3,700 miles (6,000 km) north into the Mediterranean Sea, through the mountains of Ethiopia and then the deserts of Sudan and Egypt. The river splits into two main branches and many smaller ones, creating a triangle-shaped delta between Cairo and the sea. The Nile Delta is called "Lower Egypt," and the long, winding valley to the south of Cairo is called "Upper Egypt." The vast majority of the Nile Valley is used for agricultural cultivation.

◄ *Rice farming in the Nile Delta is still done by pressing each rice plant by hand, deep into the flooded fields. The rich soils, bright sun, and abundant water allow farmers multiple harvests throughout the year.*

The Deserts

The contrast between the fertile Nile Valley and the harsh desert on either side is very striking. Apart from a few oases filled with palm trees, and impressive chalk formations, the western deserts are mostly featureless wastelands. In contrast, the eastern deserts consist primarily of rugged, rocky mountains along the Red Sea and in the Sinai Peninsula. The Red Sea beaches are a diver's paradise of coral reefs, with many rare species of coral and brightly colored tropical fish.

◀ *Unusual rock formations in the White Desert. Apart from the Nile Valley, which is only a few miles wide in many places, Egypt is a land of vast and varied deserts.*

An Arid Landscape

Despite the lush Nile Valley and Egypt's rich agricultural land, most of the country is extremely dry. The Mediterranean coast tends to have more rainfall than the rest of the country, which usually gets only one or two brief rainfalls every year. If it weren't for the waters of the Nile, the entire country would be desert, much like neighboring Libya.

IN THEIR OWN WORDS

"My name is Abdallah Abu Suliman, and my family and I live in Wadi Haggag, which is in the southern part of the Sinai. The life of the Bedouin in Sinai is very different from the old days. We have lived in the deserts for thousands of years, but life was much harder in the past. Until a few generations ago, the only way we could earn a living was to sell dried fish, dates, and charcoal from the acacia trees.

"Now, most of the Bedouin in this area work in tourism, which gives us a lot more money than before. I have four camels and have been a desert guide since the 1960s. So although life has changed a lot, I still make my living from the desert."

The Seasons

Egypt doesn't have well-defined seasons. Between April and September it is very hot—usually above 95 °F (35 °C) during the day in Cairo and the Delta region, and rising to an average high of about 104 °F (40 °C) in Upper Egypt. October and November average between 77 and 86 °F (25 and 30 °C). The winter period is cooler, with temperatures no higher than 64 to 68 °F (18 to 20 °C) in the daytime and down to 41 to 50 °F (5 to 10 °C) at night.

▲ *The hot sun is nearly always shining in Egypt, but the water from the Nile River keeps the country from being entirely desert, like the area shown above.*

Climate Change

Like most developing countries, Egypt is struggling to enforce laws controlling the environmental pollution that is contributing to global warming. Because Egypt has such a stable, dry climate, global warming will probably have less impact here than in some other countries. However, there is the threat of rising sea levels along the Delta coastline, which could flood productive farmland or increase salt content in the water table. This would make vast areas of land unsuitable for farming. Global warming could also raise sea temperatures, killing off sensitive coral reefs and jeopardizing the tourism industry.

◀ *The colorful coral reefs in the Red Sea attract many tourists, but the impact of tourism and rising sea temperatures are endangering the reefs themselves.*

IN THEIR OWN WORDS

"My name is Radi Mohamed Suliman, and I have been working at plant nurseries for ten years. The weather here in Zamalek is not as extreme as in the Delta and Alexandria, but the wind is a problem for the plants. The *khamaseens* are especially bad.

"The worst sandstorm I remember was in 1997. The sky went nearly black at two o'clock in the afternoon! After that storm, many of the branches of the plants were broken from the strong winds, and the leaves were covered with sand. The weather has changed in the last ten years. It is hotter in summer, and we recently had the coldest winter I can remember."

Sandstorms

The most unusual weather in Egypt is in March and April, when sandstorms called the *khamaseens* blow in off the Sahara desert. *Khamaseen* comes from the word *Khamseen*, the Arabic number 50, and refers to a period of 50 days during March and April when these sandstorms are most likely to occur. Usually there are only two or three per year and they last a day or two at the most. However, very bad storms can sometimes bring the big cities to a standstill because of poor visibility.

▼ *The sands carried by the* khamaseen *winds from the desert cover everything. It can be very difficult to see and breathe during a bad storm.*

4 Natural Resources

Agriculture

Until the 1970s, Egypt exported more food and agricultural products than it imported. Since then it has become one of the biggest food importers in the world because of the vast increase in its population. Foods that are grown in Egypt include vegetables such as potatoes and beans and a number of fruits, including bananas, oranges, and mangoes.

Cash crops, including sugarcane and cotton, make up about 60 percent of Egypt's agricultural output. Many farmers would like to grow rice because it is highly profitable, but it also uses a lot of water. The government is trying to encourage the farming of crops that need less water, such as wheat. These crops have minimum guaranteed prices, subsidized government loans, and decreased taxes on water usage. Although most of the meat consumed in Egypt is produced locally, Australia is a major source of beef imported by Egypt.

▲ *Sugarcane is an important crop for many farmers in Egypt, as it brings in much-needed cash to buy other goods.*

IN THEIR OWN WORDS

"My name is Nagy Khalifa, and I am an irrigation engineer at El-Maghraby Farm, south of Alexandria. Before I started work here in 1988, I was a farmer in my village, Nubareya, about 6 miles (10 km) away. In our village, we brought water directly from the canal in ditches to flood the fields with water. This farm uses a modern, computer-controlled drip irrigation system, which protects the environment. It saves a lot of water and electricity, and it protects the soil from being eroded. With water flow and other factors carefully controlled, the plants will grow better and yield more fruit. Because of the lack of arable land in our country, it's important to find ways to increase crop yields while still protecting the environment."

The Aswan High Dam

The Aswan High Dam was built in 1971, and although it has caused some environmental problems (discussed in Chapter 5), it has also delivered many benefits. The waters from the dam have been used to convert 700,000 *feddans* (a *feddan* is an ancient Egyptian measure of land still used today, equal to about 1 acre [0.42 hectare]) of farmland from annual flood-cycle irrigation to year-round irrigation. Over one million *feddans* of desert have been reclaimed. Evaporation from Lake Nasser, which stretches over 300 miles (500 km) behind the dam, has even caused rain to fall over formerly arid regions. The dam saved Egypt from ten years of drought and famine that are still being felt in Sudan and Ethiopia, and it prevented disastrous flooding in 1988. It is also used to produce hydroelectricity.

▼ *Without the electricity generated by the Aswan High Dam, Egypt would be unable to continue developing its industries.*

Petroleum

Although the petroleum industry provides jobs for only a small proportion of the population, in financial terms it is Egypt's largest export. However, this is offset by a huge and ever-increasing domestic demand for oil and other petroleum products such as gas. In 1999, despite the huge amount of crude petroleum exported, Egypt needed to import refined petroleum products because it does not have enough of its own refining facilities. Part of the problem is that the government doesn't have the money to develop the new oil fields that have been discovered in the Western Desert and the Nile Delta regions. Government incentive programs are planned to increase private investment in the development of these new oil fields and in the building and operation of new refineries.

◀ *This power plant at Al Arish on the eastern Mediterranean coast produces its electricity from burning petroleum.*

IN THEIR OWN WORDS

"My name is Mohamed Sayed and I drive an NGV (Natural Gas Vehicle). My car also runs on gasoline, so if I have problems or run out of natural gas, I can switch to gasoline. When my car was first converted three months ago, it didn't run very well, but after a few days it was fine. Natural gas is less powerful than gasoline, especially when I'm traveling at high speeds on the highway, but it is cleaner for the environment and safer for my own health. Also, the fuel is cheaper. I think that all cars in Cairo should eventually be converted to natural gas."

Natural Gas

Recently there have been discoveries of vast natural gas deposits along the Mediterranean Sea, under the Nile Delta and in the Western Desert. This means that natural gas is likely to be the key factor in Egypt's industrial and economic growth in the future. Furthermore, electricity is being generated in thermal power plants that burn natural gas rather than oil, because it is cleaner and cheaper.

Despite the vast increase in domestic consumption of natural gas, the total potential output far exceeds this demand. When all the new gas fields have successfully been tapped, and more pipelines have been built, natural gas exports will probably overtake petroleum exports in importance.

▶ *Egyptians are encouraged to use natural gas in their homes for cooking and water heating. Cooking with natural gas is good for both the environment and the economy. Where natural gas lines have not been constructed, people use bottled gas in their homes.*

Mineral Resources and Cement

Egypt has small but valuable deposits of lead, iron, and zinc in the mountains of the Eastern Desert. Its primary industrial product is cement, which is made with limestone that is also mined in the Eastern Desert. Four of the 20 most profitable companies in Egypt are cement manufacturers, and the demand for cement is constantly increasing as the need for housing and office space continues to grow. Marble and other types of building stone, such as granite, are also quarried.

◀ *The limestone in the mountains of the Eastern Desert provides an endless supply of cement for construction. Projects range from five-star hotels constructed by top international companies to local housing built by small companies.*

The Suez Canal

After many failed attempts, the Suez Canal was finally built during the 19th century. It runs from the Mediterranean Sea to the Red Sea. Apart from a brief period of war between Israel and Egypt when it was closed to traffic, the canal passes 7 percent of the world's sea trade through its waters. At 103 miles (167 km) long, the Suez Canal is the longest canal in the world without any locks. It is too narrow for large ships to pass each other in opposite directions, so traffic travels in alternating directions about every 15 hours. Also, supertankers that were designed to travel around the west coast of Africa when the canal was

closed during World War II (1939–1945) are too big to use the canal. There are plans to widen and deepen it to allow these larger ships to pass through, and to allow ships to travel in both directions at once. This would double the volume of the canal's traffic every day, and the income it provides.

▲ *Although the Suez Canal is wide in places, most of it is too narrow or too shallow for two ships to pass each other.*

IN THEIR OWN WORDS

"My name is Aly Abdel Aziz Ibrahim. I am the director of transit for the Suez Canal Authority. I've been working here since 1963 and have seen many changes. The canal has been enlarged twice since 1980. In June 2001, the largest ship ever passed through the canal, carrying half a million tons! The biggest change I've seen is the way the ships are monitored. Originally, this was done from observation posts. Each ship was registered by hand and the observer would telephone to the next post. Now we operate a modern radar system. In the future, we hope to upgrade this to a satellite system. The canal is incredibly important to Egypt's economy, and it's important that we keep up with technological developments."

5 The Changing Environment

Urbanization

Like most other developing countries during the past 50 years, Egypt has seen a vast increase in the percentage of its population living in cities. Some 46 percent of Egyptians now live in cities, and nearly one in four lives in Cairo. This change is having a dramatic effect on Egypt's natural environment.

One third of the Nile Valley is now developed, and the built-up area is growing all the time as new houses, apartment blocks, and roads are constructed. Many people in former rural areas now find themselves living in cities as their villages become part of the urban sprawl. New housing has usually been built on farmland, which means that the area devoted to agriculture in the valley has been decreasing. Since the late 1970s, however, cities have been built in the desert, which has never been farmland.

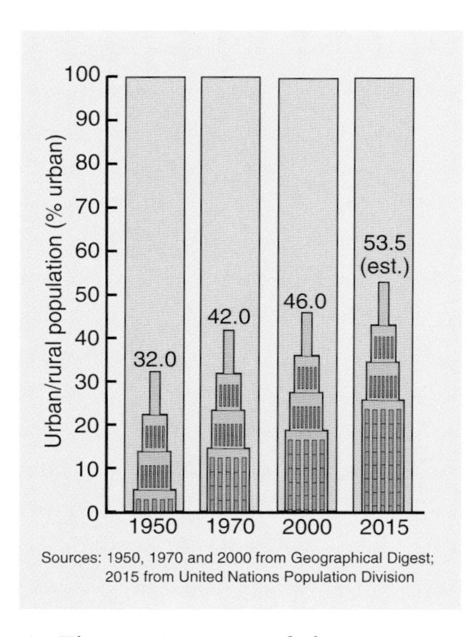

▲ *The percentage of the Egyptian population living in cities has increased rapidly since 1950, and is predicted to continue rising.*

Noise Pollution

Egyptians in the cities not only have to live with smog, but overcrowding leads to a constantly high level of noise that

◀ *Not long ago it was necessary to cross open fields to reach the pyramids from Cairo. Today the city is built right up to the edge of the desert.*

IN THEIR OWN WORDS

"My name is Isis Fathalla, and I am 72 years old. I am a professor at Helwan University. I have two daughters and four grandchildren between 11 and 13 years old. My family is from Zagazig in the Delta, but we moved to Cairo in 1948. Our old neighborhood was a very upper-class area that had many gardens. Now I live in an apartment in Manial, which is very crowded. Everything has changed so much since I was young —houses, food, communications—everything! Even though Cairo is very overpopulated and polluted now, my grandchildren do see the natural landscape when they travel outside Cairo during the holidays."

can, in turn, contribute to stress and poor health. At busy Cairo intersections the noise can reach 90 decibels, which is equivalent to a rock concert! The traffic is nonstop, 24 hours a day, and drivers honk their horns continuously.

In addition to the noise of traffic and construction at every turn, increasing use of air-conditioning units throughout the hot summer months causes a constant background hum.

◀ *Although everyone has to live with air and noise pollution, traffic police officers suffer more than most.*

Air Pollution

Air pollution from factories, cars, agricultural field-burning, and sandstorms is a constant problem for Egyptians. Cairo has the highest levels of lead pollution and suspended particles (like dust) in the world. This leads to an estimated 10,000 to 25,000 deaths every year from respiratory illness.

The government and other developmental agencies are trying to minimize air pollution with new laws and regulations. The Cairo Air Improvement Project is gathering data on smog, to warn factories on days when they should reduce their output of pollutants. Also, the government has set a target date of 2005 to have all vehicles in the greater Cairo area using natural gas instead of gasoline.

▲ *This cement factory near the city of Helwan, south of Cairo, is one of many throughout the country. Although these factories are very important to the further development of the country, they are a major source of air pollution.*

Water Pollution

The Nile is heavily polluted from food-processing plants and other manufacturing industries, and by inadequately treated sewage. Its banks and canals are also heavily infested with the bilharzia parasite, a microscopic worm that burrows under the skin and eventually causes kidney damage and digestive problems. Unfortunately, many rural Egyptians have no choice but to use stagnant water from drainage canals for cooking, cleaning, and bathing. This water can also carry

IN THEIR OWN WORDS

"My name is Zeinab Safar. I am a senior adviser for the Cairo Air Improvement Project. We are trying to reduce air pollution, but it is difficult and expensive for factory owners to move or make improvements. Only unleaded gasoline is used in Egypt now, and many cars and power plants use natural gas. However, air pollution is still very bad. Small particles in the air that are dangerous to the lungs come from burning garbage and farm waste. We hope to improve the garbage collection system, and to recycle farm waste. Solving the problem of air pollution will take time, but people in Egypt now realize how important it is."

other diseases such as typhoid, cholera, and hepatitis. Tap water in the cities is heavily treated with chlorine, but many people still prefer to drink bottled mineral water.

▲ *The Nile is the source of life in Egypt, but the water is heavily polluted and is unsafe to drink or bathe in because of disease-carrying organisms.*

Sea Pollution

The Mediterranean and Red seas to the north and east of Egypt are major shipping channels, connected by the Suez Canal. The heavy traffic leads to pollution from engine exhaust, occasional oil spills, toxic chemical leaks, and shipwrecks decomposing on the seabed. In addition, the heavily built-up resort areas along the Red Sea were not tightly controlled until the late 1990s. Many of the beaches are still unfit for swimming because of sewage that has been pumped directly into the sea.

◀ *Although the beaches and coral reefs along the Red Sea coastline are stunning, many of the resorts where visitors stay are contributing to the pollution that is making the area unfit for future generations.*

Perennial Irrigation

When the Aswan High Dam was built, the historical region of Nubia was flooded to form Lake Nasser. The creation of the lake totally changed the agricultural cycle, replacing the annual Nile flood with controlled canal irrigation.

Perennial canal irrigation has made agriculture more stable and reliable, with increased productivity. However, the dam prevents rich silt—the secret of Egypt's agricultural success for thousands of years—from reaching farmland downriver. This reduces the quality of the soil, so farmers must now rely on chemical fertilizers, which can poison the water in the drainage canals.

There is also a serious problem with the buildup of silt behind the dam. Ministry of Energy officials estimate that the entire reservoir will be filled with silt in less than 150 years. This will severely reduce the amount of water that can be stored and used for irrigation. Long-term solutions to this problem are still uncertain.

▲ *Modern technology makes it possible to fertilize large areas of agricultural land.*

IN THEIR OWN WORDS

"My name is Mohamed Hassanein, and I am the manager of the El-Maghraby Farm in the desert south of Alexandria. When I was a young boy, I worked on my father's cotton farm. I gained a college degree, and then started working here in 1988. Since then, the farm has grown from 760 *feddans* to over 7,500 *feddans*. We grow oranges, tangerines, lemons, limes, grapefruit, grapes, strawberries, beans, peas, lettuce, and herbs for Europe, the Gulf States, and the United States. We are busy throughout the year. Our customers have very high standards, so we must run a top-quality farm. We use a modern drip-irrigation system that is more efficient and environmentally friendly than the old style of flood irrigation, and we use only organic fertilizers and sprays."

The Toshka Irrigation Plan

Lake Nasser's waters are also going to be used for the controversial Toshka irrigation plan. Water is being diverted into a huge canal network that will bring life to the arid desert. The plan is intended to increase the inhabited and arable land of Egypt from 4 percent to 20 percent. However, most of the land will probably be farmed by big commercial firms, which usually provide work for fewer people per *feddan* than their smaller counterparts. Toshka is also controversial because it is costing much more to build than was originally estimated. Other projects are underway to convert more areas of desert to farmland, especially along the north Sinai coast.

▼ *The massive Toshka project may never bring the benefits that the government has promised, but in the meantime it provides thousands of jobs for construction workers.*

6 The Changing Population

Population Growth

Egypt's population has more than doubled in the past 50 years. Today, it stands at approximately 68 million, and it is estimated that it will reach 90 million by the year 2020. The high birth rate means that about 36 percent of the population is under the age of 15. The current population growth rate is above 2 percent, but the Ministry of Health is working to bring this down to 1.5 percent by the year 2005, through family planning programs.

With only 4 percent of Egypt's land inhabited, the population density in the Valley and Delta regions is nearly 6,000 people per square mile (2,000 people per sq km). In some districts of major cities, the population density is as high as 395,000 people per square mile (150,000 people per sq km). In contrast to the Nile Valley, the deserts of Egypt are sparsely populated.

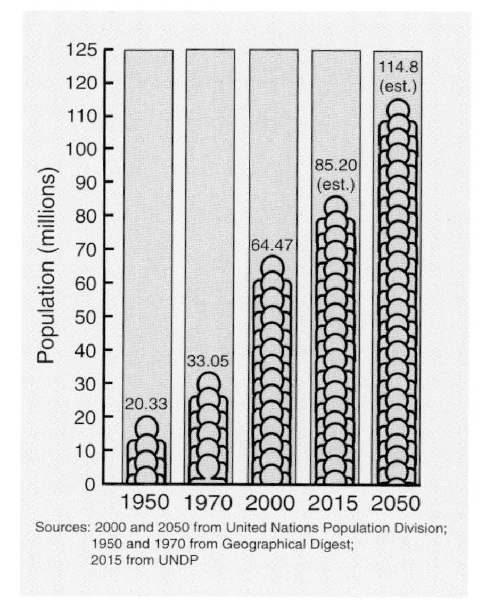

▲ *Population growth is one of the key factors of change in Egypt today, and also one of the biggest challenges for the future.*

Migration to the Cities

There are no longer enough jobs on farms in smaller towns to keep pace with rural population growth. This means that people have little choice but to migrate to the already overcrowded cities in the hope of finding work.

◀ *Approved housing is erected so quickly on the outskirts of cities that the building of quality roads, pavements, and sewers is often neglected for many years.*

Although Cairo and Alexandria are taking most of these internal migrants, Delta and Valley cities such as Tanta, Minya, and Assiyout are also seeing explosive growth.

Life is definitely better in Cairo than anywhere else in Egypt—the average household income is 25 percent higher, and the proportion of poor is 30 percent lower, than in the rest of the country. However, there aren't nearly enough jobs for all of Cairo's inhabitants. Official statistics put the number of unemployed people at about 7.4 percent, but independent estimates place the unemployment rate at between 15 and 25 percent.

▲ *New arrivals to the cities often have to live in areas where there is inadequate waste disposal and no running water or electricity.*

IN THEIR OWN WORDS

"My name is Hoda Edward Mikhail. I am the director of Physical Planning for Greater Cairo. My office is responsible for urban development in Cairo. We are improving the quality of life with better facilities and more public parks and open spaces. Migration into the city is a major problem, so one of our primary goals is to develop other regions of Egypt so that people don't need to come to Cairo to find work. Each region must provide proper facilities and job opportunities. Today, some people are actually leaving Cairo. It's not a big number, but it's increasing."

Desert Cities

As the cities grow more crowded and the need for housing rises, new cities such as 6th of October City have begun to spring up in the desert. Since the mid-1990s, the amount of land set aside for development in the desert areas surrounding Cairo totals more than one and a half times the existing land area of Cairo itself.

It can be difficult to convince people to move to these desert cities. Most Egyptians have a deep sense of connection with the Nile, and are reluctant to move to the barren desert.

▲ *6th of October City rises out of the desert sands, promising a new suburban dream for millions of Egyptians. Unfortunately, housing there is too expensive for most people.*

IN THEIR OWN WORDS

"My name is Ramadan Said and I am 14 years old. My family moved to 6th of October City from the desert oasis of Fayoum eight years ago, because there is more work here than in Fayoum.

I am in my fifth year at school. In my free time, I like to play soccer, watch television, and ride my bicycle. I have friends in Giza and Kerdassa and I like to go and see them on the weekends and during summer vacation, but I like living in this city! I hope to stay here when I grow up."

The Bedouin

The only rural people who haven't joined the general migration to the cities are the Bedouin. Although their lives have changed with modern technology such as electricity and cars, they still earn their living from the oases, their camels, and their livestock.

The Bedouin are a different ethnic group from the Egyptians of the Nile Valley. They are closely related to other nomadic Arab peoples throughout North Africa and the Middle East. Traditionally, they have tended and traded livestock such as camels and goats, and used their camels to carry goods in huge caravans across the desert trails. In the past, they lived in colorful and elaborate tents, in which the floors and walls were covered with hand-woven carpets. Modern Bedouin usually live in permanent houses in small villages around the oases and have all the benefits of modern Egypt, including schools and health care.

▼ *The Bedouin have lived in and around the oases for thousands of years, but have only recently started to establish permanent settlements.*

7 Changes at Home

Smaller Families

The average number of children in Egyptian families has been steadily dropping over the past 30 years, but there is still a big difference between urban and rural family size. Women in major cities now have fewer than three children on average, but women in rural areas usually have five or more. Many people still believe that having a lot of children is necessary, as some could die young. However, with improved health care, this is no longer common.

Birth-control education programs throughout the country attempt to reduce population growth, but it can be difficult to convince people with little education that birth control is a good idea. In the cities, where education and health care are better, the programs seem to be working.

▼ *Family size in rural areas has dropped in the last 30 years, but it is still common for women to have five or more children. In the past, an average family had more than seven children.*

The reduction of family size in the cities is a big change for today's younger generation. They may have only one or two brothers and sisters, but perhaps 10 or 15 aunts and uncles in the villages where their parents came from. With fewer children, parents have more resources per child, and can give each one more attention and provide them with more opportunities. This is particularly true for families who want their children to be well-educated. Education requires money. In many cases, private lessons are needed, as well. For the vast majority of Egyptians, this is possible only when the family has just a few children.

► *Unlike their grandmothers, these young women will probably choose to have only two children.*

IN THEIR OWN WORDS

"My name is Karim Hisham and I'm 14 years old. My family lives in Giza. I have one younger brother who is 7. Both my parents had three siblings. Most of my friends in school have only one other brother or sister. I wouldn't like to have any more brothers or sisters, as my younger brother is very annoying and bothers me all the time! After I finish school, I hope to go to the American University in Cairo. I would like to study to be an engineer, so I must do my best and get good grades. I think when I get married, I only want to have two children. That way I can make sure I give them both a good education and a comfortable life."

Better Education

Egypt's fast-growing population means that improving the education system has been a big challenge for the government. Years of neglect have left a system that discourages both students and teachers. Students' progress is based entirely on state examinations, which are held at the end of each year. The pressure to succeed in the exams is enormous, and some pupils even attempt to buy examination answers. Teachers are very poorly paid, so they often offer private lessons after school to students who can afford to pay extra fees.

In an attempt to overcome these problems, the government has invested large amounts of money in building new schools across the country, authorizing private universities, and decreasing class sizes in schools. Today, a larger proportion of Egyptians than ever—including girls—is completing school and going on to college. Only a generation ago the literacy rate of women was less than 10 percent, and it is now nearly 50 percent. Most schools and universities are still single-sex because of Islamic tradition. However, some schools, especially in the private system, are experimenting with coeducational classes.

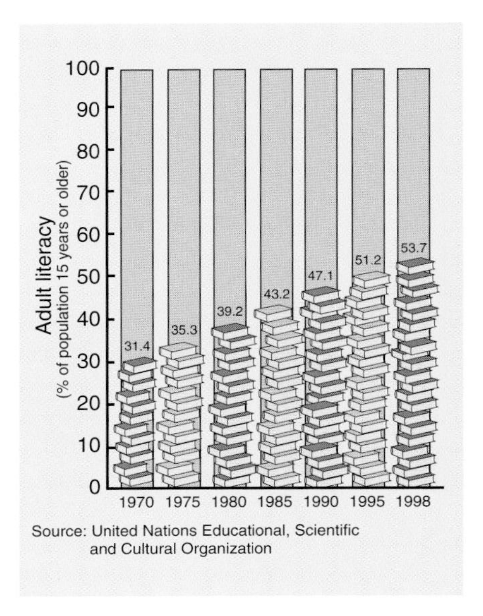

▲ *Adult literacy in Egypt is now over 50 percent.*

◀ *At this high school in Giza, boys and girls are educated together.*

IN THEIR OWN WORDS

"My name is Seba Khanna and I'm 13 years old. I'm in the front in this picture. Before we moved here, my family was living in Abu Dhabi and I went to an American school. I have always had boys in my class. I think this is a good idea because after you finish school you'll know how to live with different sorts of people.

"My mother went to a foreign language school like this one and attended Cornell University in the United States. That was very rare in those days, but now more and more women are going on to college. I hope to study journalism or communications. I definitely want to have a career when I grow up."

Leisure

The Egyptians' favorite pastime—especially for boys—is soccer. Almost everybody has a favorite team and when important games are played, the country practically comes to a standstill as everyone gathers around TV sets in their homes or in stores.

Egyptian girls have traditionally stayed at home, but today girls in the cities often play sports, visit the new shopping malls, and go to the movies. Life for young urban Egyptians today—with numerous television channels on satellite, Western films in movie theaters, and access to the Internet—is very different from just a generation ago.

▼ *Many young people today like to socialize in modern cafés like the one below.*

Diet

The traditional Egyptian diet revolves around *fuul*, a type of bean, eaten boiled and flavored with oil, salt, and lemon, or as a deep-fried bean paste called *taamiya*. Otherwise, the diet is very similar to other countries in the region and includes kebabs, rice, hummus (made from chickpeas), eggplants, and tomatoes.

▲ *A typical Egyptian meal is eaten with the fingers of the right hand.*

Most Egyptians eat mainly vegetarian meals because meat is too expensive. Chicken and lamb are the most popular meats, and although pork is forbidden for Muslims, the large Coptic Christian population and non-Muslim foreign residents can buy pork. With the growing number of foreign restaurants and large Western-style supermarkets, many Egyptians are experimenting with different kinds of food. Italian-style pasta dishes are particularly popular.

▼ *A wide variety of fruits and vegetables are available all year round in the markets of Egypt.*

IN THEIR OWN WORDS

"My name is Aia Shorosh, and I am 14 years old. At my school, they don't serve lunch, but we do have a cafeteria where we can buy sandwiches and snacks. My favorite foods are pizza and macaroni. I also like to eat Western-style fast food from places like McDonalds, Pizza Hut, and Kentucky Fried Chicken. I would rather eat a hamburger than a *shwerma* sandwich. My parents didn't have as many choices for restaurants as we have now. I guess fast food isn't very healthy, but it's different from what I eat at home. With my family, we usually eat traditional Egyptian-style meals."

Fast Food

Many Western fast food chains now have outlets in Egyptian cities, and their presence is changing the typical diet of young urban Egyptians. The food is relatively expensive by standards of the local economy, and several have waiters and try to create an atmosphere of sophistication. They are popular meeting places for teenagers and many of them also offer home delivery. Local Egyptian restaurants are now beginning to serve Western-style fast foods, which young people often prefer to traditional Egyptian fare.

▲ *Western foods such as french fries and soft drinks are now available throughout Egypt.*

Improvements in Health and Medicine

Over the past several decades, Egyptian life expectancy has increased, infant mortality has dropped, and the quality of health care in hospitals and clinics has improved. However, these achievements haven't been easy, as many Egyptians have a very unhealthy lifestyle. They smoke, eat fatty foods, and don't exercise very much. Illness is usually treated with medicine bought from a local pharmacy, often without a proper prescription.

Poor sanitation also causes constant problems with parasites and bacterial infections, such as typhoid and, in some rural areas, outbreaks of cholera and hepatitis C. It is estimated that over 40 percent of hospital admissions are related to infectious illness caused by poor sanitation.

Improving the population's health is especially difficult in rural areas, where access to health care is sometimes limited. There are now twice as many doctors per 1,000 people as there were just 20 years ago, and the number of hospitals has also increased. But most doctors don't want to work in rural areas, and clinics often can't find enough staff to meet the demand. While only 1 in 12 children in Cairo dies before the age of 5, nearly 1 in 7 dies before age 5 in the rural areas of Upper Egypt.

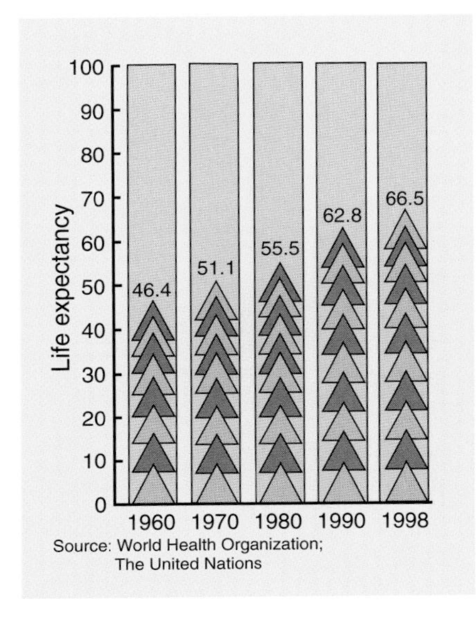

▲ *The increase in life expectancy since 1960 is an indication of improvements in Egyptian health care.*

▼ *Many Egyptian children now have regular health checkups that help prevent infectious*

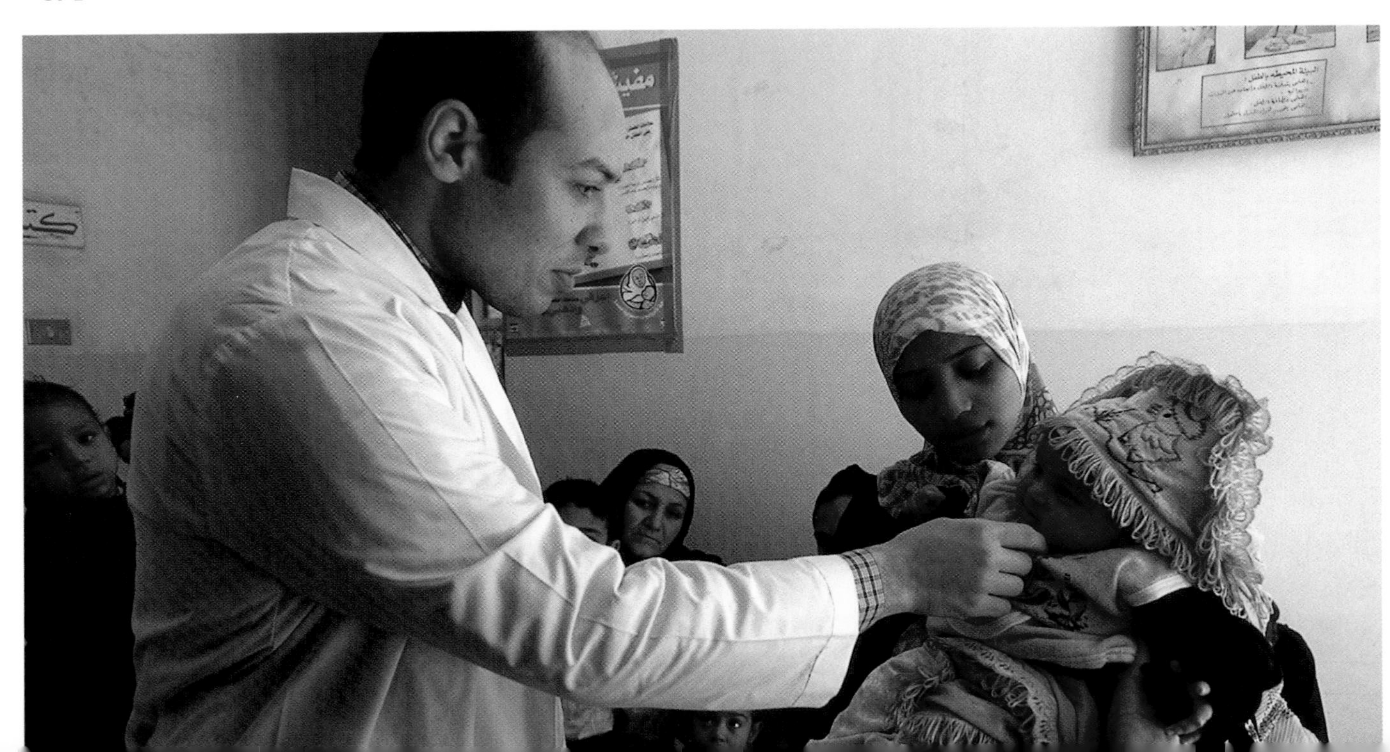

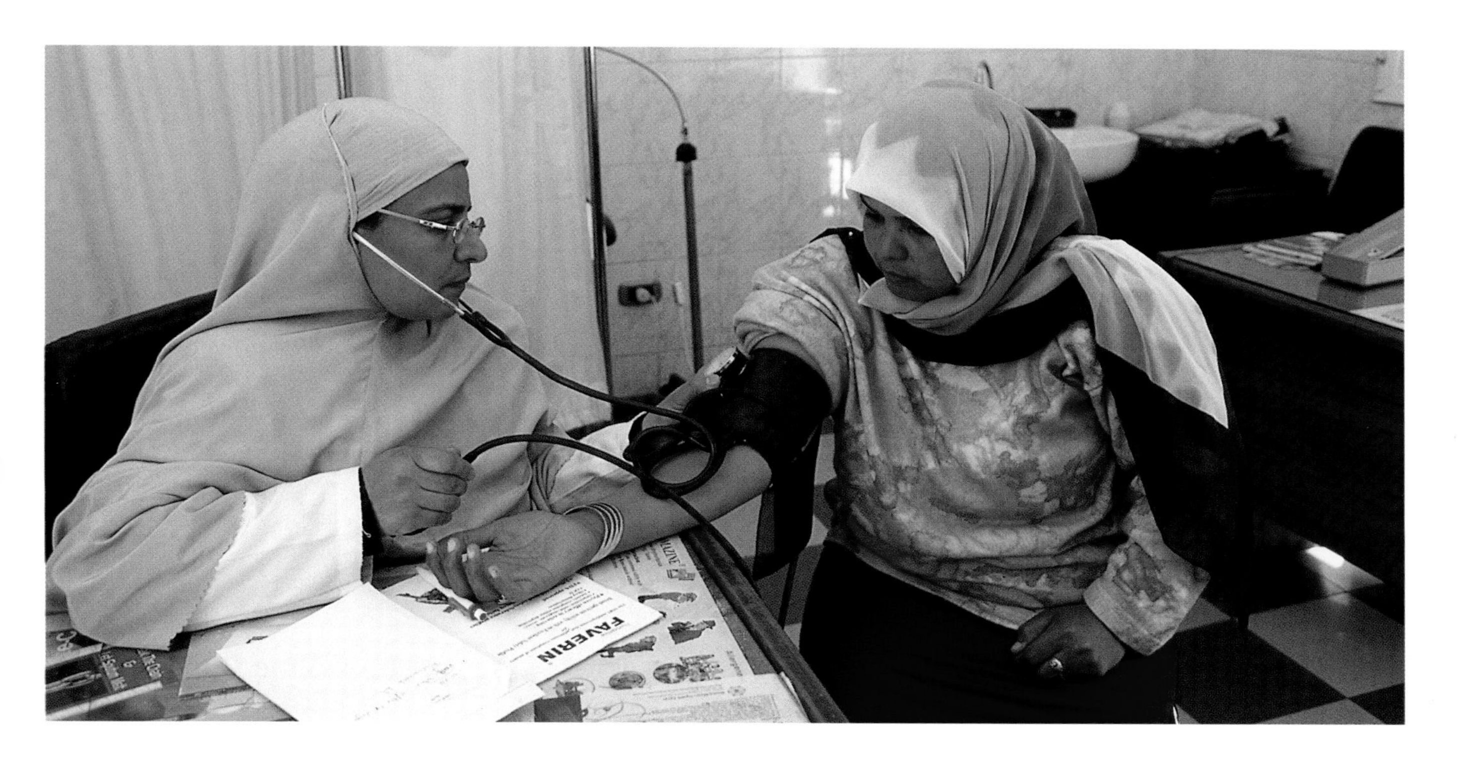

Anyone who can afford private health care will pay to go to a private hospital where the treatment is better. This is a growing problem for the government sector, because it is difficult to convince doctors to continue to work in public hospitals when the pay is so poor in comparison to the private health industry.

▲ *The increasing availablility of health care in rural areas is making a big difference in the quality of life for Egyptians.*

IN THEIR OWN WORDS

"My name is Hala Araby Bastawi and I'm 28 years old. I'm a family doctor in a public clinic in Luxor. The biggest health problems here are high blood pressure, diabetes, and intestinal disorders in adults. With children, we treat a lot of respiratory infections and diarrhea. Health in Egypt has improved a great deal in recent years. All children now receive regular vaccinations, and our clinic also has workers who go to homes to encourage good hygiene and early treatment of health problems. In general, the big difference in health problems between rural areas and the cities has to do with poverty."

8 Changes at Work

Reduced Government Bureaucracy

After independence in 1952, the government promised work for everyone and a guaranteed job in the government for every college graduate. This led to a huge, inefficient bureaucracy and very poor living standards for millions of civil servants. At present, the government is trying to reduce the size of the civil service, improve living standards, and encourage private sector employment in order to develop the general economy and qualify for continuing international aid.

For the most part, private companies now offer more opportunities for advancement and better salaries than the government. So, unlike their parents, young people no longer view government jobs as the only option. However, most college graduates still try to secure a job with the government because civil servants cannot be fired or made redundant. Reducing the size of the bureaucracy is therefore a slow process, and will only happen as current workers retire.

▼ *These businessmen in the Mohandiseen district of Cairo work for a private company that offers better pay and more opportunities than government positions provide.*

Growth of the Private Sector

New government incentives have helped create thousands of new businesses and have encouraged many foreign companies to open offices in Egypt. These private companies are in nearly all sectors of the economy—from technology and manufacturing, to retail, tourism, and transportation. The better working conditions and wages in the private sector have placed increasing pressure on the government to improve the conditions of civil servants. However, in order to increase wages for public employees, the number of employees has to be reduced even further.

► *This clothing factory in Giza is one of the many private companies that has benefited from new government incentives.*

IN THEIR OWN WORDS

"My name is Mariam Fayez and I'm the media relations coordinator for the Ministry of Communications and Information Technology. I relate the ministry's activities to the public through the media, working with members of the press. Government work in Egypt is changing. Now we are not necessarily guaranteed a job after college, and the ministries are starting to take a more businesslike approach to fill positions. I could probably make more money in the private sector, but government salaries have started to improve. Besides, I like my job. I meet key decision-makers, and the minister discusses important matters with me."

Making Ends Meet

Unfortunately, many Egyptians, especially government workers, work full-time for a salary that is too low to support a family, and must therefore undertake a second job. For well-qualified professionals, this means holding down one government job and one in private industry. For people without university qualifications, a second job is usually some form of self-employment such as driving a taxi, selling goods in the market, or transporting goods by truck.

▲ *Many people sell goods in the markets as a second source of income. You can find just about anything in an Egyptian market.*

IN THEIR OWN WORDS

"My name is Adel Shawki, and I've been driving a taxi in Cairo since 1989. Until 1996, I had two jobs. I worked at the Ministry of the Interior from 7:30 A.M. until 1:30 P.M., and drove a taxi after I finished at the Ministry until around 7:00 P.M. I needed the extra job to make enough money to support my family.

"Eventually I quit my government job and became a full-time taxi driver, which allows me more freedom and makes me more money. My financial situation has improved quite a lot since I started driving a taxi."

Working in Other Countries

Another way that Egyptian men earn money is to work in other countries, particularly in the petroleum industries of the Gulf states such as Kuwait, Saudi Arabia, and the United Arab Emirates, where salaries are much higher than in Egypt. Egyptians working in other countries now send home nearly $3 billion every year, and this is one of Egypt's main sources of foreign currency income. If the price of oil falls, many of these jobs are at risk, and people may be forced to return to Egypt and try to find work at home.

The frequency of people working two jobs or outside of Egypt means that many parents have less time to spend with their children at home. Children watch more TV, go out more with friends, and learn their values from their peers rather than from their parents. This is a big change from a generation ago.

▼ *Although working abroad often means leaving a wife and children behind, the financial rewards can benefit the whole family.*

Women at Work

Prior to independence, most Egyptian women rarely left their homes other than to go shopping for food. Today, however, the number of women working in both the public and private sectors is increasing. There are now women dentists, engineers, teachers, factory workers, and bankers.

There are still some positions, especially in the military, the police force, and religious institutions, that women are not allowed to take for traditional, religious, or legal reasons. Many women still work only until they have children, or after their children have left home. In the middle and upper classes, some professional women continue their careers and employ nannies, cooks, and housekeepers to help with domestic work.

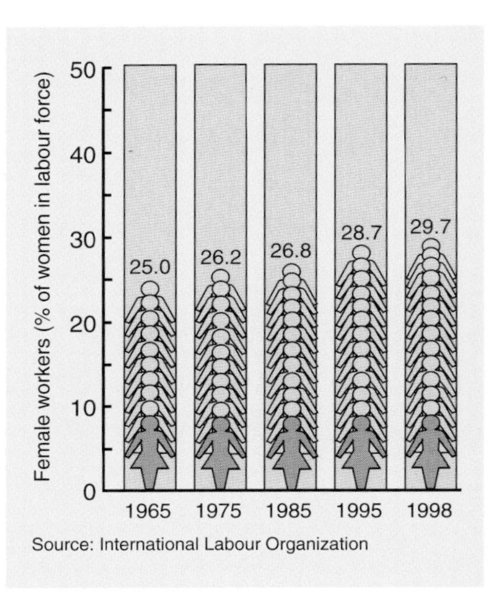

▲ *The number of women in the Egyptian workforce has been increasing slowly but surely since 1965.*

◀ *Although many women now work in private industry, they are still not paid as well as men, partly because employers assume that most women work to supplement their husband's income.*

Tourism

▲ *This stallholder is of the many Egyptians whose work is dependent on tourism.*

Although Egypt's pyramids and pharaonic sites are still the primary attraction for international visitors, the white beaches of the Sinai and the Red Sea are becoming increasingly popular with tourists. Hundreds of new hotels and resorts have been built along the Red Sea coasts and thousands of jobs have been created, many filled by formerly nomadic Bedouin herdsmen.

Although European, American, and Japanese tourists flock to Egypt by the planeload, the number of visitors is never guaranteed, because people are very sensitive to political tensions in neighboring Israel and the Palestinian territories. Whenever there is a problem in the region, the number of tourists drops dramatically, which can seriously affect the economy and employment trends.

IN THEIR OWN WORDS

"My name is May Hussein, and I'm the business development manager for Nile Online. We provide Internet services. I helped create this company in the late 1990s. The IT industry has many good opportunities for women. In this type of work, gender is less important than knowledge. I'm not married, but I'm thinking about it, and I hope to have children. I plan to keep working after I have children, although I realize that there are some challenges to being a working mother. People assume you can't do things because you're a woman and a mother. But things are changing, and it's becoming easier to be a working woman in Egypt."

Fewer Jobs on the Farms

While most of the major changes in Egypt in recent years have been in the cities, life is also changing for the *fellaheen*, the rural peasants. For thousands of years, people made their living from farming in the rich Nile Valley, and apart from occasional years of drought or excess flooding, could rely on the crops to feed their families. Today, the increasing population means it is more difficult to find work on the farms. Furthermore, with the use of tractors and combine harvesters, there is less work for traditional farm laborers.

In recent decades, most of these displaced farm workers moved to the cities to find jobs and a better life. However, government cutbacks mean that there are no longer as many jobs in urban areas as there used to be. The cost of living is so high that most people cannot afford to live in the cities while they look for work. The government is now making an effort to provide more work in the rural towns and villages, and to encourage private businesses in Egypt's smaller cities.

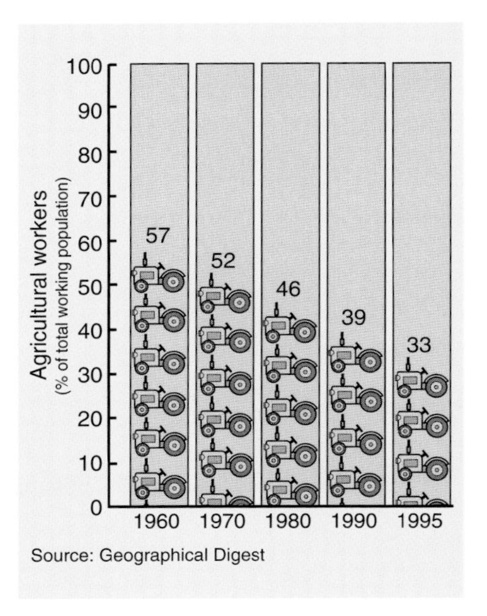

▲ *The percentage of Egyptian workers employed in agriculture has declined dramatically since 1960.*

◀ *While many farming processes have been mechanized, laborers still do most work by hand on smaller farms.*

◀ *Although there aren't enough farming jobs to support the growing rural population, many people find it too expensive to move to the cities to find work.*

Domestic Work in the Cities

Options in the city for rural migrants are limited. However, they often use family or village connections to find employment with wealthy families. One or two family members will move to the city and find work with middle or upper class families, and then slowly bring the entire family into the city to work at other domestic jobs such as doormen, cooks, nannies, drivers, and cleaners. These jobs are jealously guarded once they are found, and are often passed on from one generation to the next.

IN THEIR OWN WORDS

"My name is Ahmed Genawy and I've been a *bowaab* (doorman) at this building in Cairo for 27 years. I'm from Kom Ombo in Upper Egypt, and I came here when I was 26 years old. I have four sons and five daughters. In the beginning, it was just me taking care of this building day and night. Now I work from the morning until around 10 P.M., and I have an assistant who stays the night and keeps an eye on things. My sons also come and help during the day sometimes. When I retire, I'm going to take my family back to Kom Ombo and return to being a farmer, which is what I did before I came to Cairo."

9 The Way Ahead

Living standards have continued to improve in Egypt's cities over the past several decades, despite the overcrowding, pollution, and ongoing immigration from rural areas. Meanwhile, change is occurring at a much slower pace in the rural lands along the Nile and in the isolated Bedouin settlements of the desert oases.

Further improvements in housing, education, health care, and economic development, particularly in rural areas, are essential if Egypt is to continue to make progress in the general standard of living for all its citizens. New desert cities and modern irrigation plans are helping to ease the pressures of an ever-increasing population, and the declining birth rate in urban areas is a positive step toward slowing population growth.

◀ *These young girls playing soccer have greater freedom and more opportunities than women of older generations.*

One of Egypt's greatest assets, tourism, is also a potential problem. As more tourists visit its monuments, coral reefs, and beaches, these fragile treasures are frequently damaged. However, this is being addressed by the government, and Egypt's natural environment and historical treasures are increasingly protected.

IN THEIR OWN WORDS

"My name is Mohamed Shahata. I'm 15 years old and I've worked as a mechanic's assistant for four years. I'm happy doing this—it's much better than going to school. The money I make is helping my family.

"Things have changed a lot in Egypt since my parents were young. There are more opportunities in business, and people don't rely on the government for work as much as they used to. When I'm older I'd like to own a garage. The biggest problem Egypt has is that there are too many people. But I think families are getting smaller. I don't think I want children at all!"

Egypt is a land of stark contrasts—desert Bedouins and Nile Valley Egyptians, ancient monuments and modern irrigation works, urban professionals and rural villagers, Arab popular music and movies and religious devotion. Today's young people face new problems and new opportunities that their grandparents could not have imagined, but Egyptians face the future with optimism and an eternally good nature.

▼ *Egypt is a fascinating mix of the traditional and the modern.*

Glossary

Agriculture The industry of farming, to grow food and other plants for human use.

Annual flood cycle The rising level of the Nile every year from heavy rains in the mountains.

Arable land Land that is suitable for growing crops.

Bureaucracy A system of government involving many levels of management.

Caravan A large group of camels used to transport goods across the desert.

Commercial Anything that is used for profit-making purposes.

Consumer Someone who pays for and uses goods and services in the economy.

Coral reef Colorful, rocklike living creatures that grow on the sea floor.

Currency The money used in a country.

Decibel A measure of noise levels.

Delta The fan-shaped outlet of a large river into the sea, with many channels.

Drought A period of little or no rainfall.

Economy The system of income and expenses, employment, and production in a country.

Eroded Worn away by wind and rain

Evaporation The loss of water because of heat and sun.

Export To sell goods to another country.

Famine A time when many people are hungry or starving.

Fellaheen The rural farmers of Egypt.

Fertilizers Substances added to soil to help plants grow.

Fuul A common type of bean eaten in Egypt.

GNP Stands for gross national product, which is the total amount of money earned by all a country's business in a year.

Hummus A paste made from chickpeas.

Hydroelectric power Electricity generated by the flow of water from a dam.

Import To buy goods from another country.

Industrial To do with industry, generally manufacturing.

Irrigation Supplying water to fields of crops using ditches, canals, or sprinkling systems.

Kebab A skewer of grilled meat or vegetables.

Migration The movement of large numbers of people from one area to another.

Monsoon The time of year in many tropical areas when most of the rain falls.

Nomadic Referring to people who travel regularly and do not have permanent houses.

Oasis A small area in a desert where water is close to the surface.

Perennial canal irrigation Water from canals used on farms all year round.

Pharaoh One of the ancient kings of Egypt, who thought of themselves as gods.

Quarry An open pit in a hill or mountain that useful rocks are taken from.

Redundant To lose one's job because it is no longer needed.

Respiratory illness An illness affecting the lungs, making breathing difficult.

Rural The area of a country that is not built up into cities and large towns.

Shwerma A type of sandwich with grilled lamb stuffed into a pocket bread.

Silt Rich soil that is carried down from the mountains by rivers.

Subsidized Goods or services that are paid for partly or completely by the government.

Taamiya A paste made of *fuul* beans, shaped into balls and then deep fried.

Thermal power plants Plants that generate electricity from burning fuel, for example, petroleum.

Urban The area of country that is built up into cities and large towns.

Wastelands Land not used for anything.

Year-round irrigation Water used on farms all year round.

Further Information

Books

Bailey, Linda. *Adventures in Ancient Egypt (The Good Times Travel Agency)*. Buffalo, NY: Kids Can Press, 2000.

Ganeri, Anita. *Legacies from Ancient Egypt*. London: Thameside Press, 2000.

Harrison, Steve and Patricia Harrison. *Egypt (Landmark Series)*. London: BBC Publications, 1992.

Humphreys, Andrew and Siona Jenkins. *Lonely Planet Egypt, 6rd Edition*. Oakland, CA: Lonely Planet, 2002.

Pateman, Robert. *Egypt (Cultures of the World)*. New York, NY: Benchmark Books, 1995.

Pollard, Michael. *The Nile (Great Rivers)*. New York, NY: Benchmark Books, 2000.

Shuter, Jane. *Farming and Food (The Ancient Egyptians)*. Westport, CT: Heinemann Library, 1992.

Stein, R. Conrad. *Cairo (Cities of the World)*. Danbury, CT: Children's Press, 1996.

Videos

Mysteries of Egypt, National Geographic Video

Useful Addresses

The Embassy of the Arab Republic of Egypt
3521 International Ct. N.W.
Washington, D.C. 20008
Tel: (202) 895-5400

Egyptian Tourist Authority
630 Fifth Avenue, Suite 1706
New York, NY 10111
Tel: (212) 332-2570

Index

Numbers in **bold** are pages where there is a photograph or illustration.